BIG PICTURE 📷 SPORTS

Meet the

OAKLAND RAIDERS

BY

ZACK BURGESS

NORWOOD HOUSE 🏠 PRESS

CHICAGO, ILLINOIS

NORWOOD HOUSE PRESS

P.O. Box 316598 • Chicago, Illinois 60631
For more information about Norwood House Press please visit our website at
www.norwoodhousepress.com or call 866-565-2900.

Photo Credits:
All photos courtesy of Associated Press, except for the following: Black Book Archives (6, 7, 16, 18, 21, 22), Topps, Inc. (10 both, 11 top, 23), NFL Pro Line (11 middle), Pinnacle Brands (11 bottom).

Cover Photo: G. Newman Lowrance/Associated Press

The football memorabilia photographed for this book is part of the authors' collection. The collectibles used for artistic background purposes in this series were manufactured by many different card companies—including Bowman, Donruss, Fleer, Leaf, O-Pee-Chee, Pacific, Panini America, Philadelphia Chewing Gum, Pinnacle, Pro Line, Pro Set, Score, Topps, and Upper Deck—as well as several food brands, including Crane's, Hostess, Kellogg's, McDonald's and Post.

Designer: Ron Jaffe
Series Editors: Mike Kennedy and Mark Stewart
Project Management: Black Book Partners, LLC.
Editorial Production: Lisa Walsh

LIBRARY OF CONGRESS CATALOGING-IN-PUBLICATION DATA
    Names: Burgess, Zack.
    Title: Meet the Oakland Raiders / by Zack Burgess.
    Description: Chicago, Illinois : Norwood House Press, [2016] | Series: Big
       picture sports | Includes bibliographical references and index. |
       Audience: Grade: K to Grade 3.
    Identifiers: LCCN 2015023943| ISBN 9781599537436 (Library Edition : alk.
       paper) | ISBN 9781603578462 (eBook)
    Subjects: LCSH: Oakland Raiders (Football team)--Miscellanea--Juvenile
       literature.
    Classification: LCC GV956.O24 B87 2016 | DDC 796.332/640979466--dc23
    LC record available at http://lccn.loc.gov/2015023943

288N—072016
Manufactured in the United States of America in North Mankato, Minnesota

CONTENTS

Words in **bold type** are defined on page 24.

The Raiders celebrate a touchdown.

CALL ME A RAIDER

The Oakland Raiders always play hard. They also have fun. But nothing is more important to the Raiders than winning. That's why their fans cheer extra-loud for them. Being part of "Raider Nation" is one of the biggest thrills in the National Football League (NFL).

TIME MACHINE

The Raiders started in the **American Football League (AFL)**. **Al Davis**  built them into a championship team. After joining the NFL, they won the Super Bowl three times. The Raiders have a knack for finding imaginative players. Marcus Allen was one of the best.

Marcus Allen tries to outsmart a tackler.

Fans can watch football and baseball games at the Raiders' stadium.

Best Seat in the House

It used to be common for football and baseball teams to share the same stadium. The Raiders share their stadium with the Oakland A's baseball team. The Raiders were the first to play there. It became their home field in 1966.

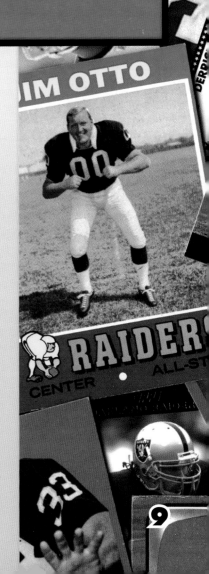

JIM OTTO
00
RAIDER
CENTER   ALL-ST
33

Shoe Box

The trading cards on these pages show some of the best Raiders ever.

JIM OTTO

CENTER • 1960-1974

Jim starred for the Raiders for 15 years. He was an **All-Pro** 10 times.

GEORGE BLANDA

QUARTERBACK & KICKER • 1967-1975

George always gave the Raiders a chance to win. He led them with his passing and kicking.

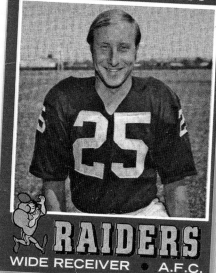

FRED BILETNIKOFF
RAIDERS
WIDE RECEIVER • A.F.C.

FRED BILETNIKOFF

RECEIVER • 1965-1978

Fred never seemed to drop a pass. He was the Most Valuable Player in Oakland's first Super Bowl victory.

HOWIE LONG

DEFENSIVE END • 1981-1993

Howie was big, quick, and very strong. No player was better at crashing through blockers.

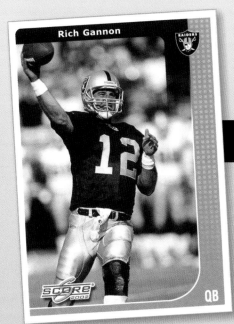

Rich Gannon

RICH GANNON

QUARTERBACK • 1999-2004

Most thought Rich's career was over when he joined the Raiders. At age 37, he passed for nearly 5,000 yards.

THE BIG PICTURE

Look at the two photos on page 13. Both appear to be the same. But they are not. There are three differences. Can you spot them?

Answers on page 23.

13

TRUE OR FALSE?

Tim Brown was a star receiver. Two of these facts about him are **TRUE**. One is **FALSE**. Do you know which is which?

1. Tim set an NFL record by returning a punt for a touchdown at age 35.

2. As a boy, Tim wanted to play for the Cleveland Browns because of his last name.

3. Tim made the **Pro Bowl** nine times for the Raiders.

Answer on page 23.

Tim Brown played 16 seasons for the Raiders.

Being a Raiders fan
can be a wild ride.

Go Raiders, Go!

Raiders fans love to wear crazy costumes. Some dress like "road warriors." Others paint themselves silver and black. The Raiders feed off the passion of their fans. It gives them extra energy when a game is on the line.

shing Overcomes Chargers

RAIDERS

Alexand

ON THE MAP

Here is a look at where five Raiders were born, along with a fun fact about each.

 1 **GENE UPSHAW · ROBSTOWN, TEXAS**
Gene was named All-Pro five times for the Raiders.

 2 **RAY GUY · SWAINSBORO, GEORGIA**
Ray was the first punter to be voted into the **Hall of Fame**.

 3 **PHIL VILLAPIANO · LONG BRANCH, NEW JERSEY**
Phil's goal-line tackle was the key play in the Raiders' first Super Bowl win.

 4 **TED HENDRICKS · GUATEMALA CITY, GUATEMALA**
Ted was nicknamed "The Mad Stork."

 5 **SEBASTIAN JANIKOWSKI · WALBRZYCH, POLAND**
Sebastian holds the team record for points scored.

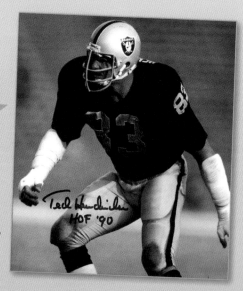

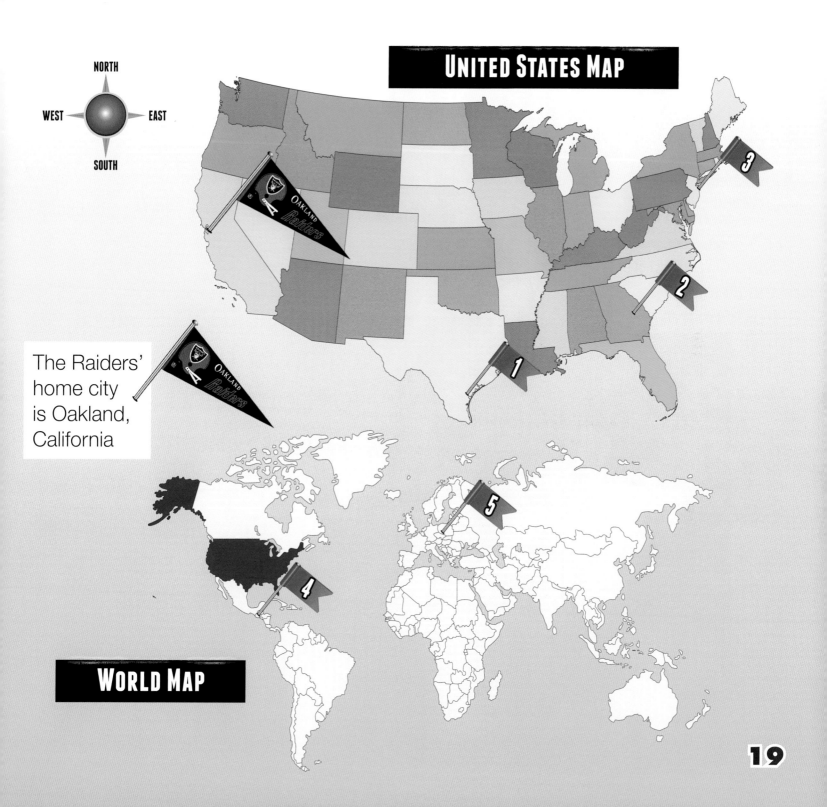

NORTH

WEST ● EAST

SOUTH

UNITED STATES MAP

OAKLAND *Raiders*

The Raiders' home city is Oakland, California

OAKLAND *Raiders*

WORLD MAP

HOME AND AWAY

Derek Carr wears the Raiders' home uniform.

Football teams wear different uniforms for home and away games. The Raiders are famous for their silver and black colors. Their uniform has barely changed over the years.

Amari Cooper wears the Raiders' away uniform.

Fans love the Raiders' helmet. It is silver with a black stripe down the middle. Each side has a shield that shows a pirate. "Raider" is another word for pirate.

WE WON!

The Raiders have played in the Super Bowl five times. They won three championships.

Those titles came in 1977, 1981, and 1984. The coach for their first Super Bowl victory was **John Madden**. He was one of the smartest coaches in NFL history.

RECORD BOOK

These Raiders set team records.

Daryle Lamonica

TOUCHDOWN PASSES		RECORD
Season:	**Daryle Lamonica** (1969)	34
Career:	Ken Stabler	150

TOUCHDOWN CATCHES		RECORD
Season:	Art Powell (1963)	16
Career:	Tim Brown	99

RUSHING TOUCHDOWNS		RECORD
Season:	Pete Banaszak (1975)	16
Career:	Marcus Allen	79

ANSWERS FOR THE BIG PICTURE
The number is missing on jersey #4, the stripe on #28's helmet changed color, and #77 changed to #67.

ANSWER FOR TRUE AND FALSE
#2 is false. Tim did not want to play for the Browns.

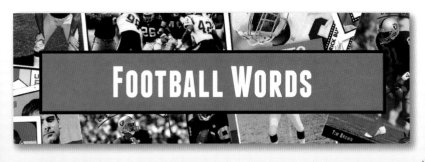

FOOTBALL WORDS

INDEX

All-Pro
An honor given to the best NFL player at each position.

American Football League (AFL)
A rival league of the NFL that played from 1960 to 1969.

Hall of Fame
The museum in Canton, Ohio, where football's greatest players are honored.

Pro Bowl
The NFL's annual all-star game.

Photos are on **BOLD** numbered pages.

ABOUT THE AUTHOR

Zack Burgess has been writing about sports for more than 20 years. He has lived all over the country and interviewed lots of All-Pro football players, including Brett Favre, Eddie George, Jerome Bettis, Shannon Sharpe, and Rich Gannon. Zack was the first African American beat writer to cover Major League Baseball when he worked for the *Kansas City Star*.

ABOUT THE RAIDERS

Learn more at these websites:
www.raiders.com • www.profootballhof.com
www.teamspiritextras.com/Overtime/html/raiders.html